My Healthy Body

SKELETON

Jen Green

ALADDIN/WATTS
LONDON • SYDNEY

© Aladdin Books Ltd 2003

Produced by:
Aladdin Books Ltd
28 Percy Street
London W1T 2BZ

ISBN 0–7496–4963–1

First published in Great Britain in 2003 by:
Franklin Watts
96 Leonard Street
London
EC2A 4XD

Editor:
Katie Harker

Designer:
Simon Morse

Illustrators:
Aziz A. Khan, Simon Morse,
Rob Shone, Sarah Smith,
Ian Thompson

Cartoons:
Jo Moore

Certain illustrations have
appeared in earlier books
created by Aladdin Books.

A CIP catalogue record for this
book is available from the
British Library.

Medical editor:
Dr Hilary Pinnock

*Dr Pinnock is a GP working in
Whitstable, Kent. She has written and
consulted on a wide variety of medical
publications for all ages.*

Contents

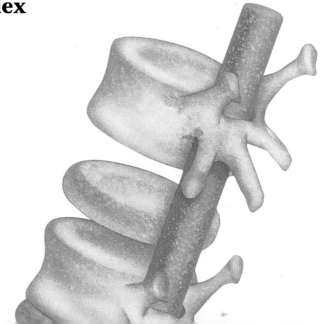

Introduction

Did you know that your body is supported by a very special framework that enables you to bend and stretch and perform all sorts of complicated movements? This special structure – the skeleton – stops you from collapsing in a heap on the floor! Your skeleton also provides protection for many of your body's vital organs. This book tells you all you need to know about your skeleton and how to keep it in good shape for a healthy body.

Medical topics

Use the red boxes to find out about different medical conditions and the effects that they can have on the human body.

You and your skeleton

Use the green boxes to find out how you can help improve your general health and keep your bones in tiptop condition.

The yellow section

Find out how the inside of your body works by following the illustrations on yellow backgrounds.

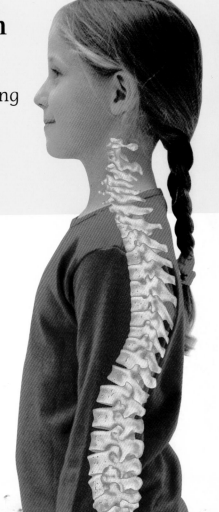

Health facts and health tips

Look for the yellow boxes to find out more about the different parts of your body and how they work. These boxes also give you tips on how to keep yourself really healthy.

The body's framework

Under your skin, most of your body parts are soft and moist, like jelly. So what keeps you in shape and allows you to move about? The answer is your skeleton – the living framework of bones that supports you and enables you to do all kinds of actions. Without your skeleton, you would collapse in a soggy heap on the ground, just like a jellyfish (right)!

Buildings have a strong but rigid 'skeleton' of steel girders to support them. Your skeleton supports you, but also allows you to move.

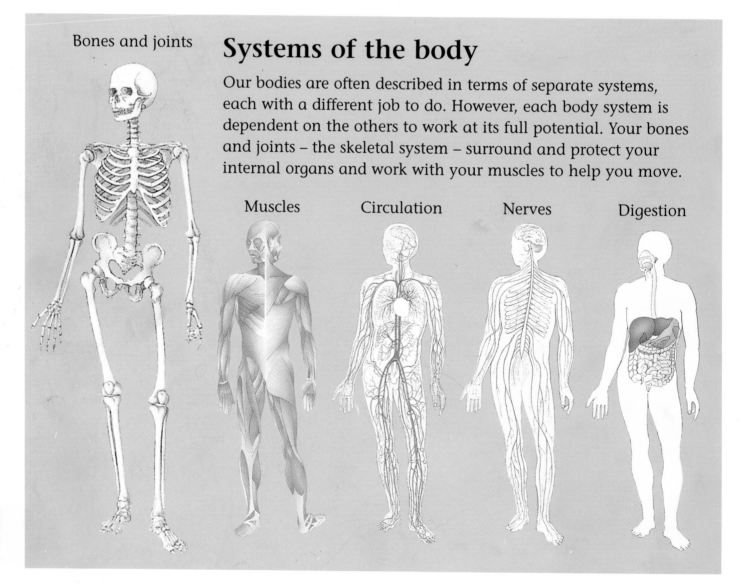

Bones and joints

Systems of the body

Our bodies are often described in terms of separate systems, each with a different job to do. However, each body system is dependent on the others to work at its full potential. Your bones and joints – the skeletal system – surround and protect your internal organs and work with your muscles to help you move.

Muscles   Circulation   Nerves   Digestion

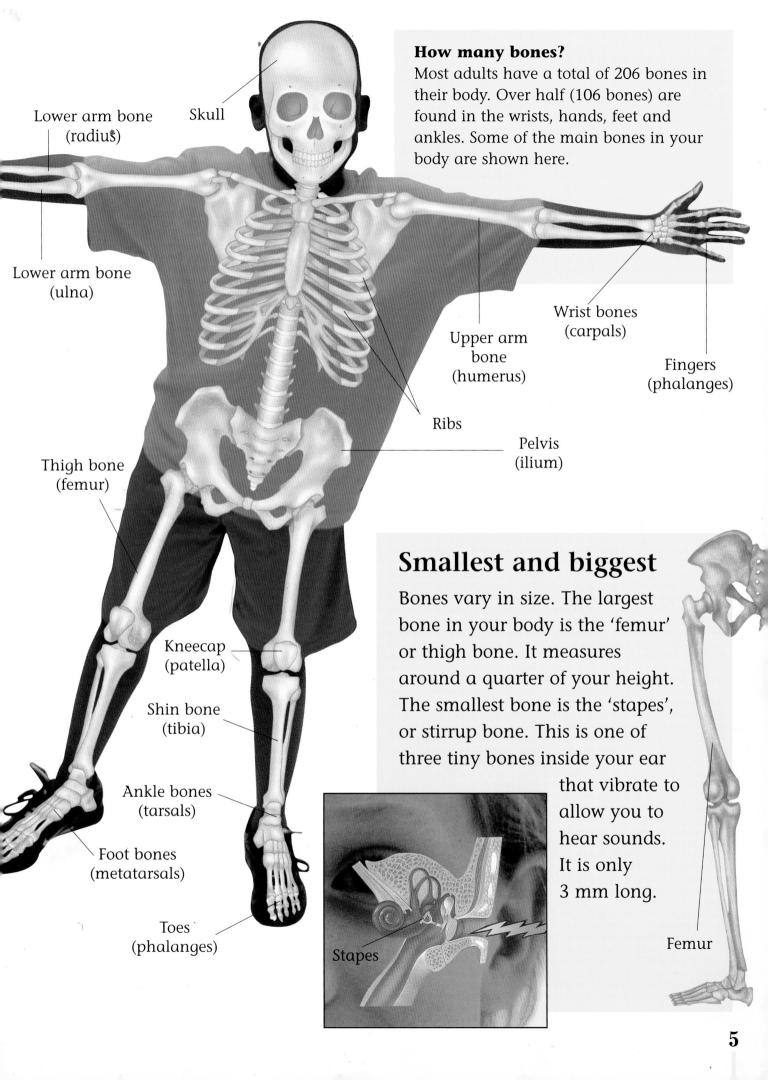

Lower arm bone
(radius)

Skull

How many bones?
Most adults have a total of 206 bones in
their body. Over half (106 bones) are
found in the wrists, hands, feet and
ankles. Some of the main bones in your
body are shown here.

Lower arm bone
(ulna)

Wrist bones
(carpals)

Upper arm
bone
(humerus)

Fingers
(phalanges)

Ribs

Pelvis
(ilium)

Thigh bone
(femur)

Smallest and biggest

Bones vary in size. The largest
bone in your body is the 'femur'
or thigh bone. It measures
around a quarter of your height.
The smallest bone is the 'stapes',
or stirrup bone. This is one of
three tiny bones inside your ear
that vibrate to
allow you to
hear sounds.
It is only
3 mm long.

Kneecap
(patella)

Shin bone
(tibia)

Ankle bones
(tarsals)

Foot bones
(metatarsals)

Toes
(phalanges)

Stapes

Femur

5

What do bones do?

X-rays and other scans enable doctors to see inside your body, to check for damage such as broken bones.

The bones in your body form a framework that is light, strong and flexible. This framework supports your body tissues and protects your vital organs. Your bones also work alongside your muscles to help you to move. Each bone in your body is a different shape, designed for different functions. For example, when you bend down to pick up a book, your leg bones act as a lever and the small bones in your hands help you to grasp the object.

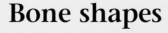

Irregular bones
e.g. spine

Flat bones
e.g. hips and shoulders

Long bones
e.g. arms and legs

Small bones
e.g. hands and feet

Bone shapes

Bones that do similar jobs often have similar shapes. For example, the long bones in your arms and legs act as levers. Flat bones, such as hip and shoulder bones, anchor the muscles. Other bones, such as parts of your spine, have an irregular shape with small 'knobs' for muscles to attach to. The small bones in your hands and feet help you to perform intricate movements and keep you balanced and agile.

Movement

Although your bones are too hard to bend, your joints allow them to move. Muscles are attached to your bones and as they contract (get shorter) your bones are pulled apart or together. Some bones move like a hinge, while others move forwards and backwards or in a rotating motion.

Protective bones

Your bones provide your body with support and protection. Your skull (below) protects your brain and forms the shape of your face. Your ribs and pelvis also form a protective cage around many of your body's vital organs.

Source of goodness

Your bones are also an important source of vital nutrients for the body. Calcium is stored in your bones and released when your body needs it. Your bones also contain a substance called bone marrow, which makes most of the blood cells that flow around your body.

Bone names

Many bones have common names. All bones have scientific names that are understood by scientists and doctors. For example, the shoulder blade is often called the 'scapula', and the collar bone is called the 'clavicle'. The 'funny bone' is not actually a bone at all (or funny) but a nerve on the outside of your elbow.

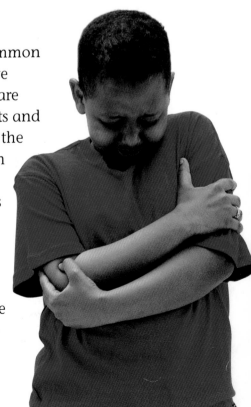

What's inside bones?

Although your bones come in many different shapes and sizes, they share the same basic structure. Bones are not solid all the way through but honeycombed with spaces, which make them light. Your bones are made up of water, minerals and protein. Minerals give your bones strength and protein makes them flexible. Bone is a living tissue that constantly breaks down and reforms.

Tough outer layer of compact bone gives your bones a strong structure.

Spongy inner layer makes your bones light.

Bone marrow produces red blood cells.

Blood vessels bring nourishing minerals to your bones.

Periosteum forms a skin to give your bones a protective layer.

Bone parts

The long bones in your arms and legs have a tube-like structure, with a hard outer layer and a softer inside. The outer layer is made of tough, compact bone. The inner layer has holes like a sponge, filled with cells and fluid. A jelly-like material called bone marrow is found in the centre. Bones are covered with a 'skin' called periosteum and are linked to blood vessels.

Cartilage

Some parts of your body's framework are made of a rubbery, gristly substance called cartilage. There are three types of cartilage. One kind forms the framework of body parts such as your voice box and outer ear. Another is an elastic tissue that thinly covers the ends of bones. The third forms connective tissues between bones like the vertebrae of your spine.

Food for bones
Your bones need small amounts of natural substances called vitamins and minerals to stay strong and healthy. The mineral calcium helps to keep your bones and teeth strong. Babies and young children need calcium to harden their bones as they are growing. Calcium is found in milk and other dairy products. Eating a healthy and varied diet should give you all the vitamins and minerals that you need to stay healthy.

Leukemia

Leukemia is a form of cancer that affects the blood. If you have leukemia, the bone marrow (right) inside your long bones loses its ability to produce normal blood cells. This makes your body less able to fight viruses and infections. Leukemia can affect both children and adults. Symptoms include frequent nose bleeds, aching bones and joints and generally feeling tired. Treatment using radiation therapy, blood transfusions and bone marrow transplants can relieve the symptoms and, in some instances, may cure the disease.

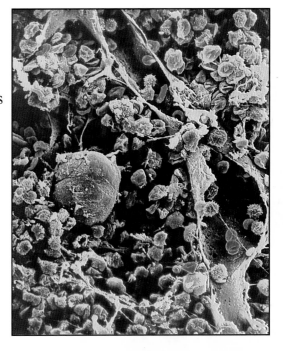

Between the bones

When joints such as elbows are overused, they can swell and fill with fluid. This is sometimes known as 'writer's elbow'.

Bones themselves only bend slightly. It is the parts where bones meet – the 'joints' – that enable you to walk, run, play sports and dance. There are three types of joints in the body – fixed joints, cartilaginous joints and synovial joints. Movement occurs where your muscles are linked to your bones across a joint, such as your elbow. When these muscles contract (get shorter) and relax, you can bend and straighten your arm.

Inside the knee

Your knee is a synovial joint where your thigh bone (femur) meets your shin bone (tibia) and your kneecap (patella). It is the body's hardest working hinge and can also rotate a little from side to side. The femur and tibia are connected by ligaments (fibrous tissues) and the patella is held in front of the joint by muscles and tendons. An area of fatty tissue and spaces between the bones (bursa) are filled with fluid that contains nutrients and prevents friction between the moving parts.

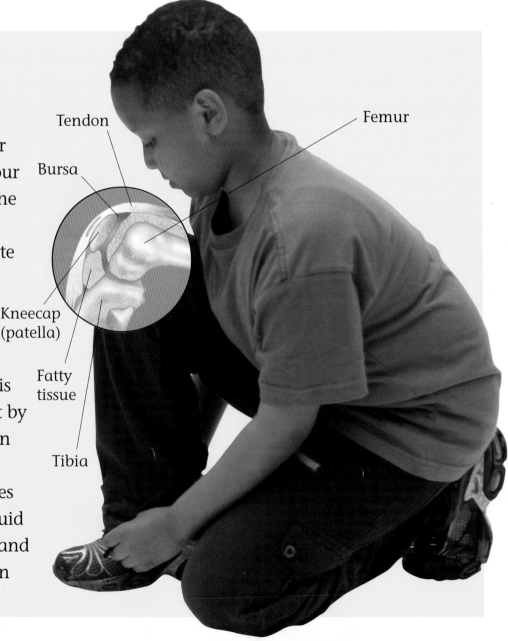

Tendon

Bursa

Femur

Kneecap (patella)

Fatty tissue

Tibia

Inflamed knees

A sudden twist or blow to the knee can cause ligaments or tendons in the joint to stretch and become inflamed or torn. If you injure or strain your knees through overuse, they may become swollen (below) as excess fluid lubricates the joint. Warming up and stretching your leg muscles before exercise will help to relieve the pressure on your knees when you start moving.

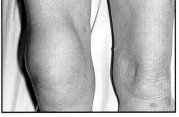

Fixed joints

Fixed joints are designed to move very little or not at all. Your skull bones are linked by fixed joints. The edges of the bones are jagged and fit together like pieces of a jigsaw puzzle, which form a protective case to hold your brain. Other fixed joints are found where your pelvis joins your spine and where your top ribs join your breastbone.

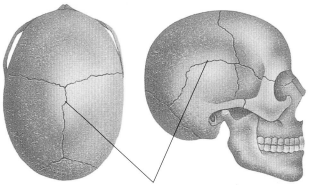

Fixed joints

Cartilaginous joints

Cartilaginous joints connect your ribs to your breastbone and your spine. In these joints, the bones are separated by a disc or strip of cartilage, called costal cartilage. These joints only move a little.

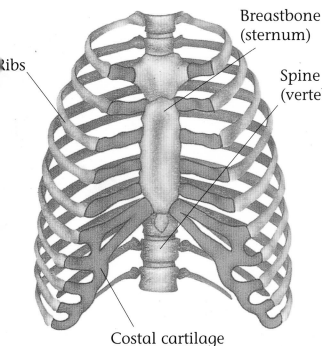

Ribs

Breastbone (sternum)

Spine (vertebrae)

Costal cartilage

Synovial joints

Synovial joints, like your knee, finger, neck and hip joints, move much more freely than other joints in your body. Tough straps, called ligaments, hold your bones together while your muscles pull on your bones. The ends of the bones are coated with slippery cartilage so they move smoothly. Synovial joints also contain a liquid called synovial fluid, which lubricates (oils) the moving parts like oil on a bicycle wheel.

Keep up the exercise

Joints need to be moved regularly to keep them flexible. If you ever have to rest an arm or a leg you will soon notice that your joints start to stiffen. The solution is to take regular exercise. Remember to warm up carefully, and to start with gentle exercise. As you become more fit, you will discover just how much you can do!

Moving freely

Your jaw is one of the strongest hinge joints in your body. It allows you to do things like chew lots of tough toffees!

Synovial joints in your body allow your arms, legs and other body parts to carry out particular movements. Hinge joints in your knees and fingers allow a forward and backward motion. Pivot joints, such as your neck, give a rotating motion. Ball-and-socket joints in your hips and shoulders allow your limbs to move freely in many directions. Ligaments hold these joints together while your muscles pull on your bones.

Sports injuries

Joint injuries can happen in the heat of a match, when players collide or limbs are twisted out of position. You can sprain a knee, wrist or ankle if you stretch or tear the ligaments that hold your bones together. Most of these injuries get better without any treatment. Rest the joint for a few days, pack it with ice and compress it with a bandage to help ease the discomfort and swelling.

Synovial joints

Synovial joints can be grouped according to the way that they work, allowing a certain kind of movement. In each type of joint, the ends of the bones are shaped and fitted together in a particular way. This ensures that the bones can move smoothly in one direction or another.

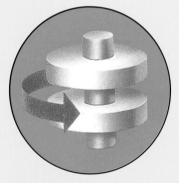

Pivot joint

A pivot joint in your neck allows you to turn and twist your head from side to side. In a pivot joint, the bony spike of one bone fits through the hollow ring of another and pivots around it.

Hinge joint

Hinge joints in your fingers, toes and knees allow the bones to move backwards and forwards, although they can only move up to a certain point. The elbow has both hinge and pivot joints.

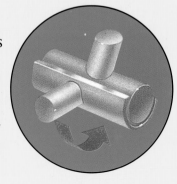

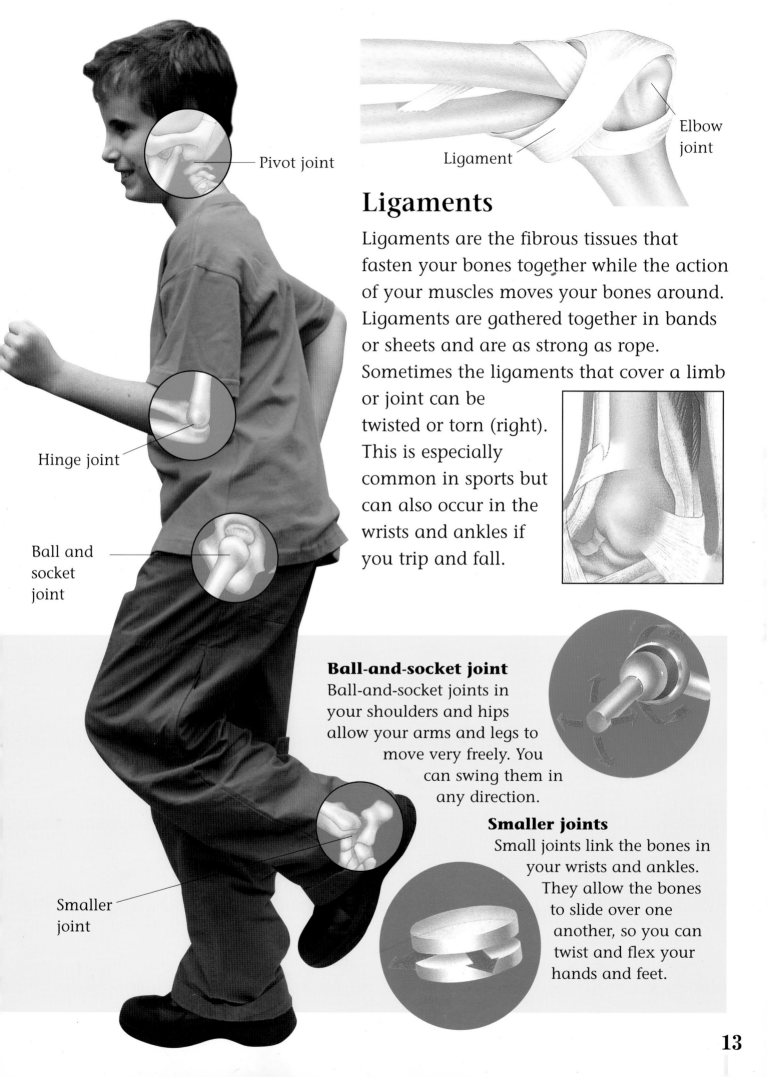

Pivot joint

Ligament

Elbow joint

Ligaments

Ligaments are the fibrous tissues that fasten your bones together while the action of your muscles moves your bones around. Ligaments are gathered together in bands or sheets and are as strong as rope. Sometimes the ligaments that cover a limb or joint can be twisted or torn (right). This is especially common in sports but can also occur in the wrists and ankles if you trip and fall.

Hinge joint

Ball and socket joint

Ball-and-socket joint

Ball-and-socket joints in your shoulders and hips allow your arms and legs to move very freely. You can swing them in any direction.

Smaller joints

Small joints link the bones in your wrists and ankles. They allow the bones to slide over one another, so you can twist and flex your hands and feet.

Smaller joint

The spine

Your spine, or backbone, provides the central support for your body. It allows you to stand upright and bend in different directions. Your spinal cord, the main bundle of nerves that connects your brain with the rest of your body, runs through openings in the bones of your spine. Your backbone prevents the spinal cord from being injured.

Spiny sections

Your spine is made up of small, wedge-shaped bones called vertebrae, which fit together to form a long, bony column. There are twenty-six bones in all: seven vertebrae in your neck, twelve in your upper back, and five in your lower back. There are also two bones at the base of the spine called the sacrum and coccyx. The sacrum is made up of five fused vertebrae and four more form the coccyx.

Spinal injury

A severe spinal injury, after a car accident or a bad fall, may damage the spinal cord. If the spinal cord is cut, nerve signals are unable to pass from the brain to other parts of the body. This causes total or partial paralysis below the level of the injury. However, some injuries to the back do not damage the spinal cord at all.

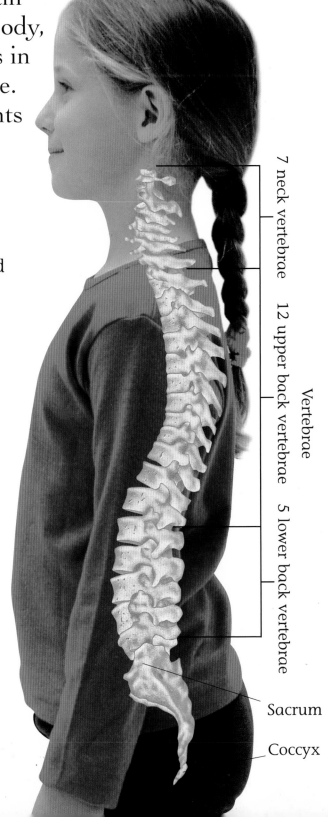

7 neck vertebrae

12 upper back vertebrae

Vertebrae

5 lower back vertebrae

Sacrum

Coccyx

14

Spine make-up

Vertebrae have a unique knobbly shape that allows them to do several different jobs at once. Holes in this chain of bones line up to form a channel for the spinal cord to go through. Disks of jelly-like cartilage between the vertebrae act as shock absorbers preventing the bones from rubbing each other. Bony spikes anchor muscles that allow you to flex and bend your back.

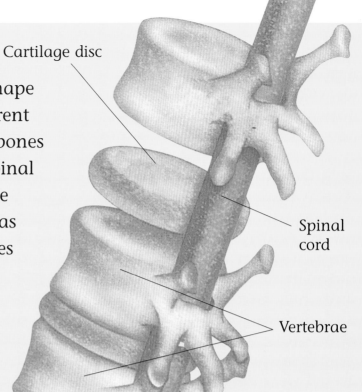

Cartilage disc

Spinal cord

Vertebrae

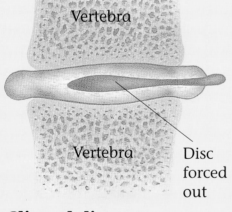

Vertebra

Vertebra

Disc forced out

Slipped disc

Bending or lifting a heavy weight awkwardly can lead to a painful condition called a slipped disc. Uneven pressure on the cartilage discs between the vertebrae can cause the jelly-like centre of the disc to become distorted and protrude. It may then press on a nearby nerve, causing sharp pain.

Good posture

Keeping your spine as straight as possible when you are standing, sitting, walking or carrying heavy items, helps to prevent back problems. The spine has a natural curve that helps to support your weight. If you slouch, you will cause your spine to curve abnormally. This stretches ligaments and, over time, can distort the discs between your vertebrae.

Bones of the head

The smallest bone in the body is the stapes in the middle ear. The size of a grain of rice, the stapes transmits sounds to the inner ear.

Your skull is made of 28 bones. Eight bones in the top of the skull (the cranium) protect your brain from injury. Fourteen bones in the face protect your sense organs, such as the eyes and nose. Muscles attached to these bones allow you to smile, talk and eat. Six bones in your ears conduct sound vibrations to your ear drum. The temporal bone, surrounding the ears, is one of the hardest bones in your body. It protects the tiny organs inside your ear.

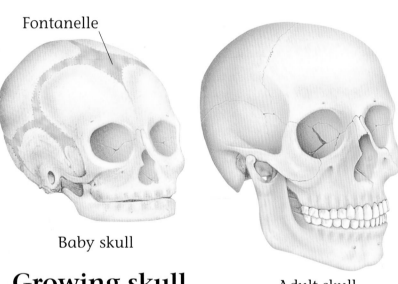

Fontanelle

Baby skull

Adult skull

Growing skull

The bones of a baby's skull have spaces between them called fontanelles, or 'soft spots'. These make the skull of an unborn baby flexible, allowing it to squeeze down the mother's narrow birth canal when it is born. The fontanelles are covered by a tough membrane that protects the baby's brain. The skull bones grow and knit together by the time a baby is 18 months old.

Unconsciousness

The bony case of the skull shields the brain from bumps, but a very hard knock can damage the skull and brain. If you have a bad head injury you should see a doctor, particularly if you feel sick or faint. If you come across a person who has received a blow to their head and is unconscious, you should not move them as this could cause further injury to their neck or spine. Keep them warm and call for an ambulance immediately.

Movement of jaw

The lower jaw bone is the only moving joint in your skull. It is connected to the fixed upper jaw by a strong hinge joint. The lower jaw moves up and down freely so you can open your mouth wide and also bite down forcefully. The lower jaw also moves a little from side to side, allowing you to chew your food thoroughly.

Wear a helmet

Canoeists, rock climbers and cyclists all wear helmets to protect their head from injury. Modern helmets are comfortable and lightweight. Always wear your helmet when you are cycling or doing an activity that could damage your head if you fall. You should always replace your helmet if it gets a hard knock.

Brain case

All the skull bones that make up an adult's head, except for the lower jaw bone, form a rigid structure. These bones have fused (grown together) during childhood to form a hard, zigzag joint called a suture.

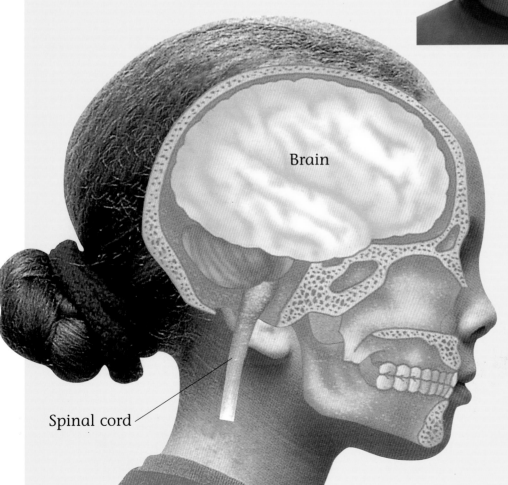

Brain

Spinal cord

Face bones

The bones that form the framework of your face are joined at sutures (immovable joints). Your eyes are protected by bones that form deep sockets (hollows). Two small bones form the bridge of your nose, while the end is supported by cartilage. The tiny bones of your ears lie inside the head where they can perform delicate movements to aid your hearing and balance.

The trunk

The bones of your body trunk (or core) include your ribs, spine, pelvis and hips. The ribs curve around to form a bony cage that protects your heart, liver and lungs. Your rib cage is also designed to move, so you can breathe in life-giving oxygen. The pelvis forms a bony ring that protects your bladder, intestines and other important parts. The hip joint is the largest ball-and-socket joint in the body and gives your legs a wide range of movement.

The rib cage

The rib cage is a springy case formed by your curving ribs, that protects your vital organs. Each rib is a thin, flat bone, semicircular in shape. At the front, strips of cartilage join the ribs to the breastbone (sternum) and make the rib cage flexible. At the rear, the ribs are attached to the spine. Most people have twelve pairs of ribs.

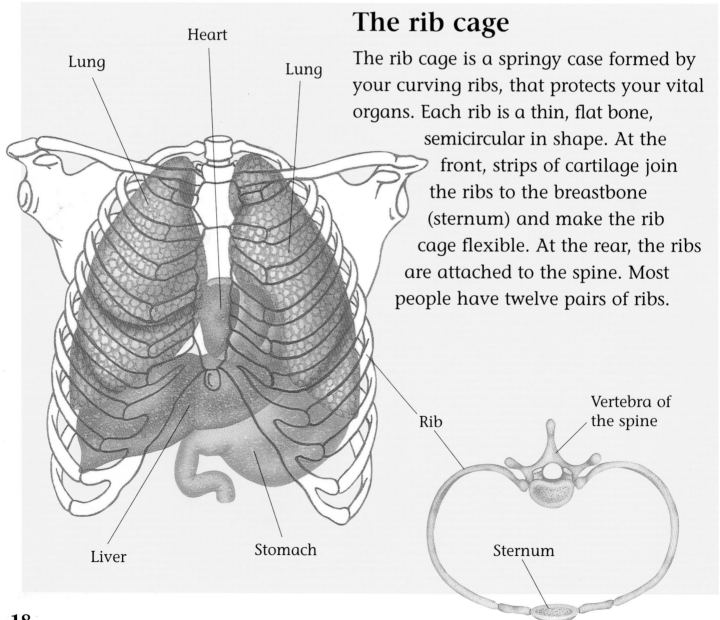

Heart

Lung

Lung

Rib

Vertebra of the spine

Liver

Stomach

Sternum

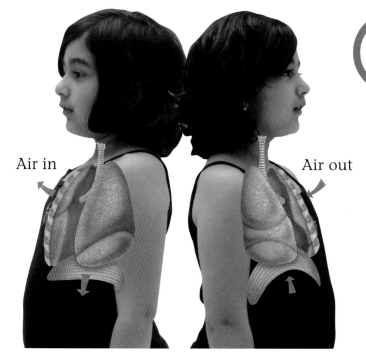

Air in   Air out

Breathing in and out

You have muscles between your ribs and a large, flat muscle, called a diaphragm, attached to the bottom of your rib cage to help you breathe. When you breathe in these muscles tighten, pulling your ribs up and outward. This makes the rib cage bigger and causes the lungs to open and fill with air. When the muscles relax, the ribs move down and inward, squeezing the stale air out.

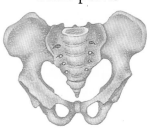

Coccyx

Human beings evolved from ape-like creatures millions of years ago. Experts believe that the coccyx, a few tiny bones at the base of your spine, is all that is left of the long tail which once helped our distant ancestors to swing through the trees. If you fall on your coccyx, it can be very painful but it is rarely permanantly damaged.

Hip joints

The hip joint is between the thigh bone (femur) and the pelvis. The head of the femur fits into a cup-shape in the pelvis to form a ball-and-socket joint. It provides movement in all directions. A few children are born with a hip socket that is too shallow – the ball on the end of the femur does not stay in the socket. This is called 'congenital dislocation'. Sometimes, in old age, the joint can become weak and break. In such cases, the joint can be replaced with a metal ball and an artificial plastic cup socket (below).

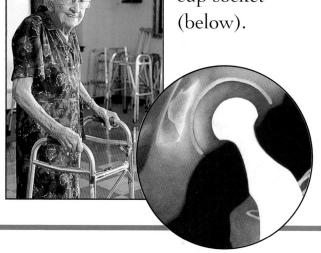

The pelvis

The pelvis helps to transfer your upper body weight to your legs so that they can balance and carry your weight as you walk and run. The pelvis has a slightly different shape in men and women. A man's pelvis is tall and slim, while a woman's is broader, which makes it easier for babies to be born.

Female pelvis

Male pelvis

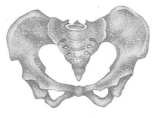

Shoulders, arms and hands

The long bones in your arms allow you to stretch to reach distant objects. The joints in your shoulders, elbows, wrists and fingers help your arms to move freely. From the shoulder to the tips of your fingers, the arm is an amazing structure. It allows you to grip, push, pull, and also perform delicate tasks such as drawing and building models.

Your arms move more freely than your legs because of the way that your joints are arranged. You can grip things tightly, like javelins, and also throw them a long way.

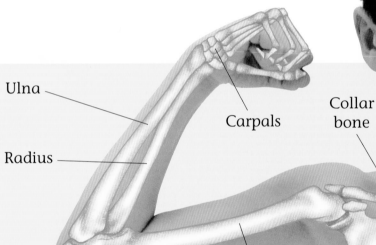

Ulna

Radius

Carpals

Collar bone

Humerus

Scapula

Arm bones

A stout bone called the humerus forms your upper arm, while two thinner bones, the radius and the ulna, support the lower arm. The top end of the humerus forms a loose ball-and-socket joint with your shoulder blade (scapula) and collar bone. The delicate collar bones hold your arms clear of your rib cage, so that you can rotate them freely.

Repetitive strain injury

Repetitive strain injury (RSI) is a painful condition that results from making small movements repeatedly. It often affects factory workers or office workers using computers. You can also injure your shoulder, elbow and wrist joints if you play sports that put a strain on one arm, such as tennis and badminton. Taking regular breaks and doing stretching exercises will ease stiff joints.

Handy bones

Although your hand is fairly small, it contains a total of 27 bones. Eight small bones in the wrist make a very flexible joint. Five long bones fan out from the wrist to support the fingers. Each finger has three bones, while the thumb has two. This complicated structure allows you to carry out a wide range of tasks, such as writing and playing the piano.

Thumb

Index finger

Middle finger

Ring finger

Little finger

Carpals

Phalanges   Metacarpals

Elbow joint

Your arm is made up of three long, strong bones hinged at the elbow. The position of the bones at this joint enables you to rotate as well as flex your arm. This movement can be seen most clearly in the hand-to-mouth motion of eating.

Delicate work

Humans are one of the few species that can move their thumb to touch each finger in turn. This special action allows you to pull on a rope, grip a hammer and carry a heavy bag. You can also perform all kinds of delicate actions, from tying a shoelace to threading a needle, writing your name, using a knife and fork and unscrewing a jam jar.

21

Legs and feet

The bones and joints of your legs and feet are tough and strong to support the weight of your body. They are also flexible enough for you to perform a huge range of movements – from crouching down or doing a long jump to hopping on one leg. You use the bones of your feet for standing and walking. Without all the bones of the foot working together, it would be impossible to balance properly.

Walking upright on two legs allows you to have a good view of your surroundings. Most other mammals walk on all four limbs.

Phalanges

Metatarsals

Tarsals

Cigarettes and alcohol

Smoking and drinking too much alcohol can affect the density of your bones. This is because smoking decreases the amount of calcium in your bone cells. Reduced bone density, or osteoporosis, makes bones brittle and more likely to break or fracture if you have a fall.

Ouch! New shoes
Uncomfortable, tight-fitting shoes can hurt and damage your feet. Wearing the right shoes for running and other sports will help you avoid blisters and sprains. So give your feet a break by wearing shoes that fit just right!

Foot bones
Your foot contains 26 bones, arranged like the bones in your hand. But the foot bones are broader and sturdier, so they can carry your weight. Five long bones fan out from the ankle bones to form the sole of your foot. Attached to these are fourteen long bones that make up your toes: two bones in the big toe, and three in each of the other toes. Seven ankle bones from a flexible joint linking your foot to your lower leg bones.

Back injuries can cause paralysis if the spinal cord is damaged. Wheelchairs provide mobility and wheelchair sports (right) help to keep bones and muscles healthy. Today, many wheelchair users take part in international sporting competitions.

Legs and feet

Like your arms, your legs have three main bones. The femur, or thigh bone, is the thickest and heaviest bone in the body. It joins your pelvis at the hip joint and your lower leg at the knee joint. Two slimmer bones, the tibia and the fibia, run from the knee to the ankle. The sturdy tibia (shin bone) and the slender fibia connect to the ankle. The tarsal bones below your ankle, form an arch shape that help you spring forward as you run. The metatarsal and toe bones in your feet help to distribute and balance your weight when you move.

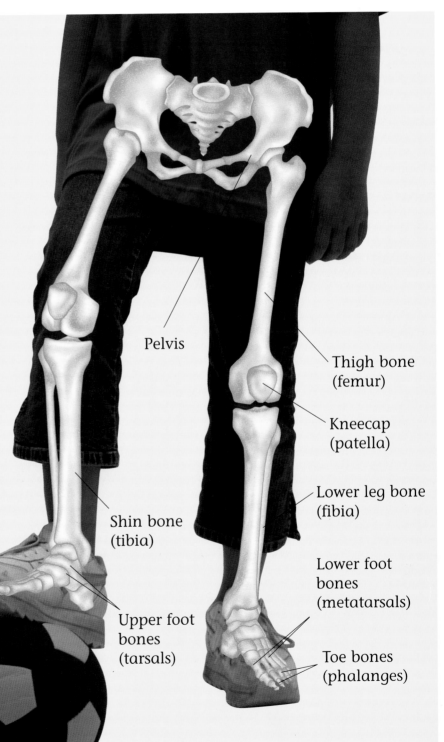

Pelvis

Thigh bone (femur)

Kneecap (patella)

Lower leg bone (fibia)

Shin bone (tibia)

Lower foot bones (metatarsals)

Upper foot bones (tarsals)

Toe bones (phalanges)

Growing and ageing

A newborn baby usually weighs between three and four kilograms. By the time a child has reached 12 years old, it usually weighs about 10 times more than its birth weight. This massive transformation of your whole body comes about mainly through the growth of your bones – especially in the arms and legs. Most growth for boys and girls happens between 10 and 16 years of age.

Babies and toddlers grow very fast in their first few years. Most babies double their birth weight by the age of 5 months !

Growing bones

When you are born, your bones are very flexible. The ends of your long limb bones are separated from the main bone shaft by a layer of cartilage. As you grow older, this cartilage layer grows and gradually fuses the parts of your bones together so that they get longer.

Baby
The bones in a baby's skeleton begin to harden and become more rigid at about eight weeks old.

Adult
You reach your full height in your late teens, but your bones and skeleton continue to change throughout your life.

Child
Between the ages of ten and sixteen, most children grow very fast. This is called the adolescent growth spurt.

Growing proportions

A baby's head is very large in proportion to the rest of the body. At birth it forms about one-quarter of its total height. During childhood, the rest of the body grows to 'catch up' – first the trunk has a growth 'spurt', then the arms and finally the legs. In an adult, the head is

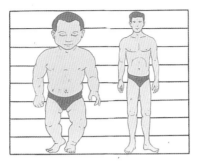

only about one-eighth of the total height. Although girls grow faster than boys, everyone grows at slightly different rates. Don't be unduly worried if you are shorter or taller than some of your friends.

Keeping bones strong

Young bones are tough and supple. As you get older, your bones gradually become more brittle, so they break more easily. This is because bone tissue is destroyed more quickly than it can be replaced (below). A good diet with plenty of calcium will help to maintain bone tissue. Weekly exercise such as jogging, athletics or football will also help to keep bones in good shape.

Thinning bone

Healthy bone

Arthritis

Arthritis is a disease caused by inflammation of the joints. Osteoarthritis generally affects the elderly and results from wear and tear on joints such as the hips and knees. Adults, and occasionally children, can develop rheumatoid arthritis, affecting the smaller joints, such as the hands (below), causing pain and stiffness. Treatments can help to ease the discomfort.

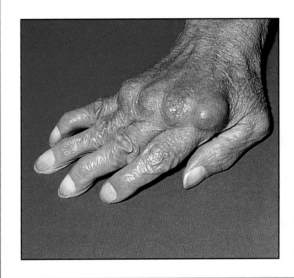

Regrowing bones

Luckily, most broken bones heal themselves and grow back to more or less how they were before the break. If a bone does not heal by itself it can be mended with a bone graft or a special treatment that uses electrical currents to stimulate bone growth. Fractures tend to heal faster when you are young, because your bones are still growing.

25

Mending broken bones

In 1975, lightning struck an English cricket umpire, fusing solid the metal joint that had been implanted in his leg, so he couldn't move!

Bones are strong and long-lasting, but they do break if they are hit too hard or get bent or twisted out of position. Amazing as it seems, bones generally mend themselves in about six weeks. Badly broken bones are set in a plaster cast to hold them still while they heal. In some cases, damaged hips and knees can even be replaced with metal joints. When a bone is broken in several places, doctors may wire or pin the bones together.

Simple fracture
In a simple fracture, the bone breaks cleanly, and the two pieces stay more or less in line.

Breaking a bone

A broken bone is called a fracture. Some fractures are worse than others. Greenstick and simple fractures are less serious than compound fractures, which take longer to heal.

Greenstick fracture
In a greenstick fracture, one side of the bone bends like a green, growing twig, while the other side breaks. This type of fracture only occurs in children, because their bones are still flexible.

Compound fracture
In a compound fracture, the bone snaps and moves out of line, piercing the skin as it does so.

Mending the leg

A broken bone heals itself in several stages. The fracture tears the bone's blood vessels so they bleed. A clot then forms to stop the flow. Bone cells and blood vessels grow across the fracture and close it. Cartilage forms and slowly hardens into bone. Scar tissue is reabsorbed and the bone returns to its normal shape.

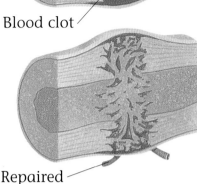

Blood clot

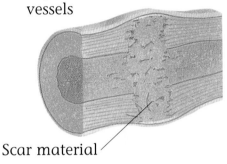

Repaired vessels

Healed bone

Scar material

Bad breaks

Sometimes a broken bone does not heal by itself. It may be broken in several pieces and will need more support than a plaster cast. Doctors may wire or pin the pieces together for proper healing (right). These pins are often removed when the bone has finally healed.

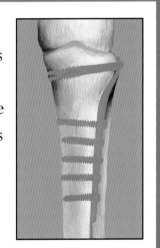

Getting plastered

Broken limbs are supported so that the bones heal in the correct position. If you break an arm or a leg, it will probably be set in a plaster cast. Splints and slings are also used to support bones while they mend.

Avoid accidents

Be careful! Watch where you walk, and wear sensible shoes. It can be easy to twist or break an ankle when wearing high heels or platform shoes. Alcohol and drugs can affect your coordination and balance and may make you dizzy, trip or have an accident. Stay clear of alcohol and drugs and keep your feet firmly on the ground!

Staying healthy

Your bones and skeleton are vital to the health of your whole body. As well as providing support and protection for softer tissues, your bones store important minerals. Bone marrow makes essential blood cells, including white blood cells, that fight off disease. You should look after your bones carefully by eating the right foods, getting regular exercise, and checking out any problems.

If a tin man does not oil his joints he will rust and cease to work. You also need to 'oil' your joints by eating healthily and exercising regularly!

Bone experts

Your doctor is able to treat sprains and many minor bone problems. Sometimes, you may need to be referred to a specialist bone doctor, called an orthopedist (below), or a rheumatologist who treats joint diseases. Other bone practioners include osteopaths and chiropractors, who treat back and other skeletal problems by massaging and moving bones, and physiotherapists who work to strengthen damaged muscles and bones.

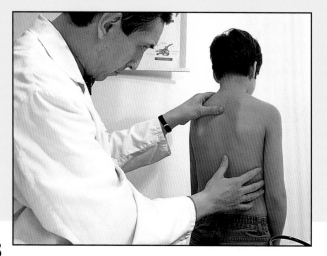

Plenty of exercise
Bones rarely wear out but sometimes older people, especially women, suffer from osteoporosis, causing their bones to become weak and crumbly. One of the best ways to avoid this is to get regular exercise at least four times a week. Exercise improves bone strength, reduces the risk of osteoporosis, and leads to better overall health.

Stronger bones
Weight-bearing exercise enables your bones to adapt to the impact and pull of your muscles by building more cells and becoming stronger. Weight-bearing exercises include walking, jogging, football and dancing. Try to do these activities a few times a week!

Minerals for bones

Certain foods supply minerals, vitamins and other nutrients that your bones need to grow and repair themselves. Eating a diet that is rich in calcium and vitamin D is important to maintain healthy bones. Fish, such as sardines, and dairy products, such as milk, yoghurt, and cheese, provide vitamin D and calcium. You also need plenty of fresh fruit and vegetables; high-protein foods, such as eggs, for strong muscles; and carbohydrates, such as rice or pasta, for energy.

Limbering up

Before vigorous exercise you should always do some warm-up exercises. Stretching gets the muscles and joints working smoothly. After exercising, you should also cool down with more stretches.

The right kit

You don't need a lot of equipment for exercise such as walking. However, for many sports you need the right clothing. This can include helmets, protective knee and elbow pads, and special boots or shoes. Playing some sports without the right gear can lead to injury, especially to your head, so make sure you are always properly equipped.

Amazing facts

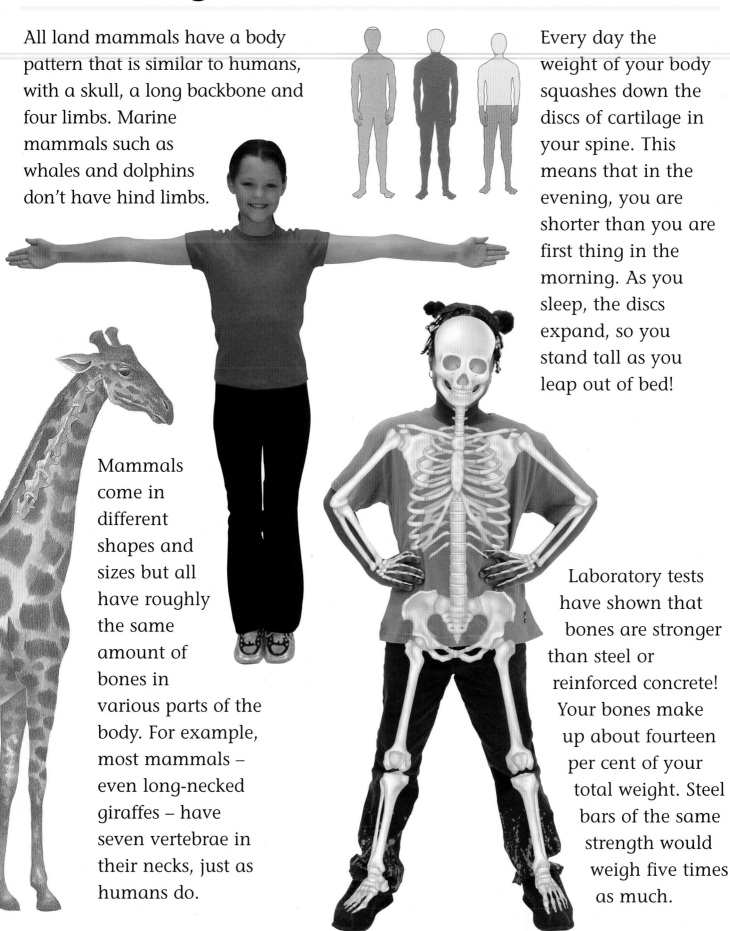

All land mammals have a body pattern that is similar to humans, with a skull, a long backbone and four limbs. Marine mammals such as whales and dolphins don't have hind limbs.

Mammals come in different shapes and sizes but all have roughly the same amount of bones in various parts of the body. For example, most mammals – even long-necked giraffes – have seven vertebrae in their necks, just as humans do.

Every day the weight of your body squashes down the discs of cartilage in your spine. This means that in the evening, you are shorter than you are first thing in the morning. As you sleep, the discs expand, so you stand tall as you leap out of bed!

Laboratory tests have shown that bones are stronger than steel or reinforced concrete! Your bones make up about fourteen per cent of your total weight. Steel bars of the same strength would weigh five times as much.

30

Glossary

Bone marrow The spongy material found inside bones. Bone marrow stores minerals for the body and produces blood cells.

Cartilage A gristly, rubbery substance that forms part of the body's framework.

Cartilage disc A disc of jelly-like cartilage that sits between the vertebrae of the spine, to prevent the bones from rubbing together.

Compact bone The hard, smooth outer layer of a bone, that gives it a strong structure.

Fracture A broken bone.

Joint The point where two bones meet. Joints include synovial joints, fixed joints and cartilaginous joints.

Leukemia A form of cancer that affects the blood.

Ligament A tough band that holds the bones of a joint together, when muscles pull on bones to make them move.

Paralysis A loss of feeling and muscle power in part of the body. Paralysis is usually caused by damage to the nerves. Spinal injuries that damage the spinal cord can lead to paralysis.

Posture A position of the body. Bad posture can cause back problems.

Skeleton The body's support framework made mainly of bone.

Spinal cord The main bundle of nerves that connects the brain with other parts of the body. The spinal cord runs down through the openings in the bones of your spine.

Spine The backbone that provides the central support for the body. The spine is made up of 26 wedge-shaped bones, called vertebrae.

Spongy bone A honeycomb-like layer inside bones. The spaces in spongy bone make bones lightweight.

Tendons The long, stringy cords that attach muscles to bones.

Vertebrae The small, hollow, irregular bones that make up your spine.

Index

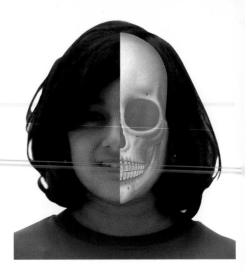

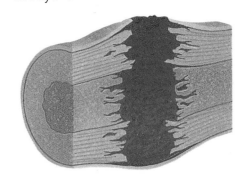